FRED & WOODY'S · FANTASTIC WORLD ·

OUR UNCLES
THE CRUNCLES

**A story for kids about love,
relationships, families and
fighting a giant squid**

Written & Illustrated by
Alex Waldron

This is the Fantastic World of Kernow County.
It is home to brothers Fred and Woody
and their family.

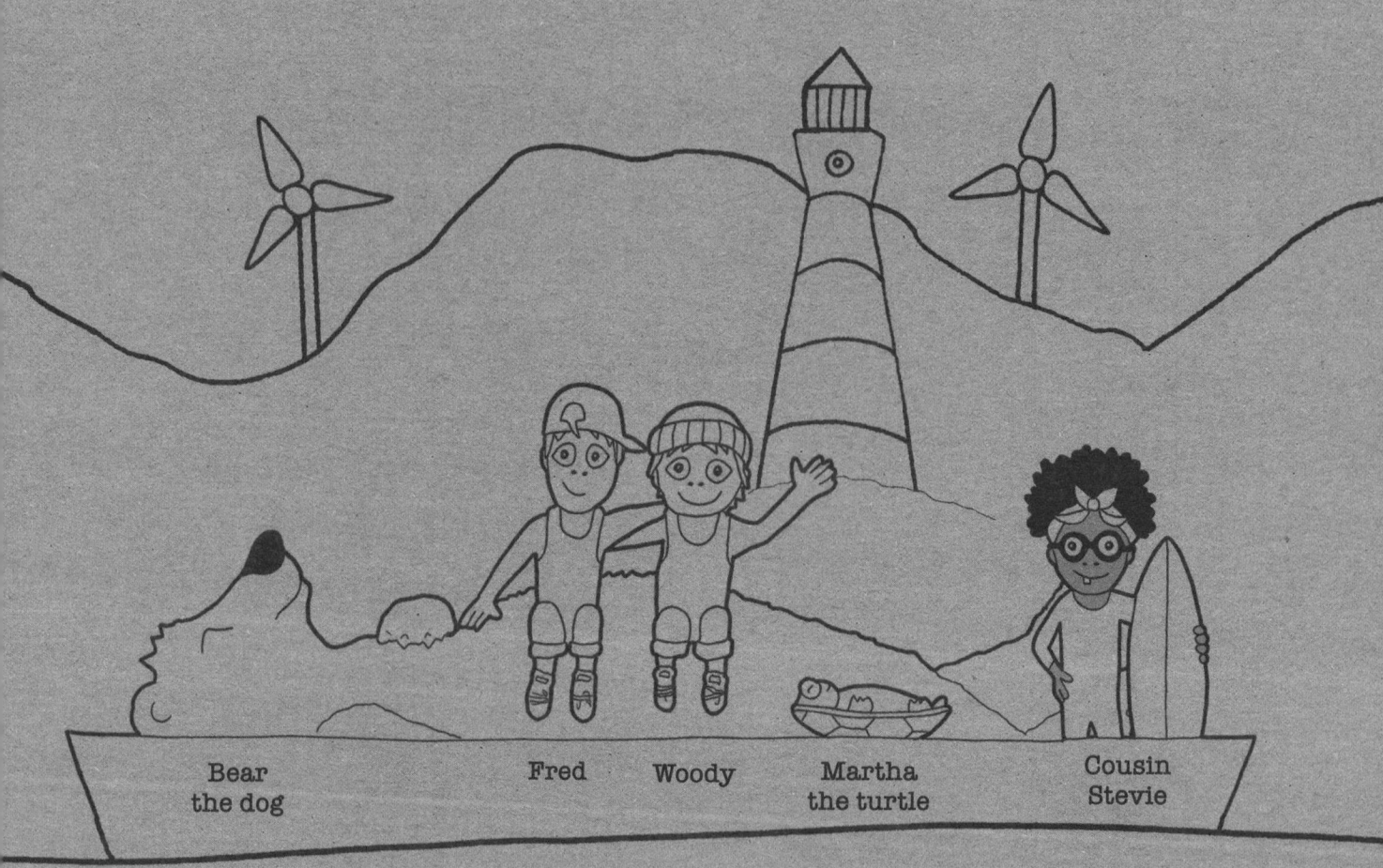

Bear
the dog

Fred

Woody

Martha
the turtle

Cousin
Stevie

And this is the tale of Fred and Woody's heroes, their amazing uncles . . .

. . . THE CRUNCLES.

Big Nan
and PooPops

Gary
Cruncle

Greg
Cruncle

Our uncles the Cruncles,
Are our heroes of the sea.

They're courageous and wise
And as funny as can be.

They squabble and quibble,
Quarrel and compete. . . .

Who has the best TACKLE?

What should they EAT?

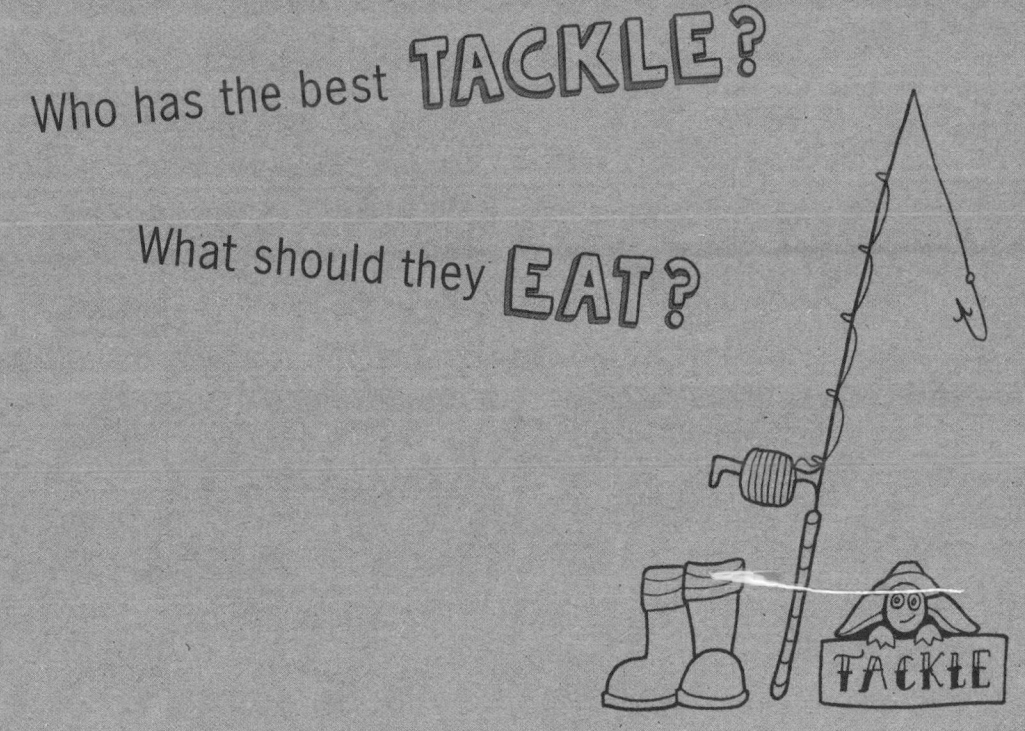

They live on a boat of adventure and travel,
Singing sea shanties with voices of gravel.

They're tough and they're rugged,
Each as strong as an ox.

Their arms covered in stories,
Their hands rough as rocks.

7

Our uncles the Cruncles,
Tell tall tales of the sea,
How they sailed out further
Than any had been.

Their bravery took them
Where others did not dare.
Deep in the darkness of
The giant squid's lair.

They battled and fought 'til
The Sun went down.

Then wearily returning
To Nevafishey Town,
They cared for their wounds
And ate hungrily,
A candlelit supper of calamari.

Our uncles the Cruncles,
To them we both turn,
When we need advice or
There are knots to be learnt.

From their onboard veg patch they grow their own grub.
And pickle and smoke it to sell to the pub.

They power their boat by
The rays of the Sun.

And fix their inventions
When they no longer run.

They are fearless and kind
And need only each other.

Like Woody and me,
But they are not brothers.

Our uncles the Cruncles,
They kiss and hold hands.
Like Mum and Dad,
Or PooPops with Big Nan.

They break up, they make up,
They laugh and they dance.
All the time looking for
A little romance.

Thick as thieves and joined at the hip,
They're each other's rock,
That no one can chip.

Through the ups and the downs
And the storms of the sea,
Their friendship and love
Are as strong as can be.

For together they're stronger,
Their hearts interlocked.
Guiding their course through
The reefs and the rocks.

19

Our uncles the Cruncles,
For all the tales that they've told,
Have taught us the most
Important lesson to hold.

Love does not choose who
It ties in a knot.

There's SOMEONE
For EVERYONE
On this fantastic blue dot.

Love does not care if you're
A pirate or sailor.

An astronaut, a doctor,
A baker or tailor.

Wedding Day

Honeymooning

First Home

Our uncles the Cruncles,
Have found their shipmate.

From the moment they met
On that awkward first date.

Whoppers

Nap Time

To the time they fell out,
Making each other blubber.

And then gently made up,
Saying sorry to each other.

Our uncles the Cruncles,
Are our heroes of the sea.
They show us each day
What LOVE can be.

The rough and the smooth,
The highs and the lows.

Their boat will sail
Wherever the wind blows.

It may steer them towards
Unexpected lands.

But they'll navigate together . . .

... While still holding hands.

BIG NAN KNOWS
IMPORTANT STUFF FOR GROWN-UPS!

Our Uncles the Cruncles has been carefully written to give you lots of opportunities to talk with young children about healthy relationships – in all their varied and wonderful forms!

All About Role Models

It's very important for kids to have good, positive role models as they grow up. A role model is someone who will guide them and whose traits they will want to imitate. Kids will also recognise and look for these traits in people with whom they form future friendships and relationships.

The Cruncles – Gary and Greg – are Fred and Woody's heroes. They are also great role models because of all the everyday things they do that Fred and Woody get to observe and experience. The Cruncles enjoy their work and work as a team. They fish, surf, grow vegetables and cook calamari. The Cruncles love their family and like it when the boys help out around the boat. They teach the boys how to tie knots and sing sea shanties but they also listen to the boys' worries and fears and are always there for them. The Cruncles are loving and kind, funny and wacky, brave and wise, creative and reliable. They are each other's "rock" and they make Fred and Woody feel safe, too.

Today, there are many "influencers" and "celebrity couples" on social media, dishing out photoshopped images and sponsored links to all the things you never knew you needed! It's more important than ever for children and young people to have REAL, positive role models in their everyday lives.

Let's Talk Role Models
Talk to your little ones about role models. What traits would you like a role model to have – for example, compassion, kindness, integrity, warmth, determination or creativity? Can you think of good role models together? Do you agree with each other? Ask your little ones why they admire their role models and discuss their choices positively. Explain why you admire your role models.

Building Emotional Resilience

The Cruncles show us that it is fine to disagree within a relationship, even to quarrel and fall out (sometimes) – as long as you then apologise and make up. Dealing with the ups and downs in relationships helps build emotional resilience.

In order for children to understand how to navigate healthy, honest and respectful relationships of their own, it is important to talk about how and why disagreements happen – and most importantly – demonstrate that it is possible to mend things. Being able to repair a relationship when we've fallen out with someone is a skill best learnt through observation and experience.

If differences really can't be resolved, then it's important to behave respectfully and to expect people to treat you with respect, too. Sometimes friendships and relationships end and we can usually learn something about ourselves or human nature from that experience. However, this should not destroy our self-esteem or make us fear making new friendships and relationships.

If a relationship is a constant battle, or either of you or those around you are hurt or upset by it, this is not healthy and you may need support. (Please see our website for useful links: www.fredandwoody.co.uk)

Let's Talk Emotional Resilience

Try talking to your little ones about a quarrel you had with someone that upset you, but that you were able to make better (no need to share all the details). Did you apologise? Did you accept an apology from the other person? How did it make you feel – for example, angry, sad, regretful or happier once you made up?

Understanding Emotional Literacy

The Cruncles are very good at expressing their feelings for each other by kissing and holding hands, caring for each other's wounds or having a good blubber. Even their quarrelling and quibbling shows they feel secure enough to disagree with each other at times. . . Then they apologise and make up. They are emotionally literate.

What is emotional literacy? Simply put, it's understanding our feelings and emotions, and those of others, and finding appropriate ways of processing and expressing them.

How can we help kids to be emotionally literate? To be honest, little ones are often pretty good at naturally expressing their feelings. But the family and culture we grow up in can affect which feelings are encouraged or discouraged. As kids get older, they may need some help to understand some of their feelings and how to express them appropriately.

Let's Talk Emotional Literacy

Try talking to your little ones about the feelings and emotions you are experiencing. This will help children to learn and understand emotional cues, develop empathy and feel safe in expressing their own feelings.

What feelings are encouraged or discouraged in your family or culture? For example, you may encourage physically expressing your love for each other through hugs. Perhaps you discourage showing anger, when sometimes we need to let off some steam to show that something has upset us.

Ask a child to name a feeling and why they feel it – for example, "I feel angry because my friend has taken my ball" or "I feel scared because my sister shouted at me". This will aid a child in recognising the feeling another time (maybe in similar circumstances), thereby understanding themselves better. Or they may recognise the feeling in another person, which develops empathy.

Try drawing gingerbread people together and then ask the child to show you on the drawing where they "feel" an emotion in their body. Emotions are often subconsciously felt in our bodies before we are consciously aware of them. Feeling prickles up the back of the neck, butterflies in the stomach or weak at the knees can all indicate emotions that are sometimes difficult to express.

Butterflies in the stomach = nervous excitement

Jelly legs = fearful feeling

WHAT IS LOVE, BIG NAN?

When Fred, Woody and their cousin Stevie asked me that question, it got me thinking.
A fair few people have tried to unravel the mystery of "What is Love?" – from the ancient Greeks
to Shakespeare and Ed Sheeran!

On pages 16 and 17, we learn that Gary and Greg are a couple and that they are in love.
But understanding and describing love can be tricky. Here's what I told my little ones,
and it might help you to discuss this topic, too. . . .

When you kids are tired and snuggled up on the sofa with me or PooPops, what do you feel like inside?

Warm. Cosy. Safe. Happy. Fuzzy. Content. Like I can just be ME!

Well . . . that sounds like love. And how do you feel about Martha and Bear the Dog?

I just want to be with them all the time. I want them to be happy. I'd do anything for them. I want to cuddle up close to them. I don't even mind walking Bear in the rain because it makes him happy!

Well, that sounds like love, too! How do you feel when you are with your uncles the Cruncles?

Treasured. Happy, Excited. Safe. Special. Confident. Brave.

Well . . . that sounds just like love! These are all feelings of love for your family and your pets. You may feel something like this for some of your friends, too.

Yes! I can't wait to see my best friends. I miss them so much when I don't see them. Sometimes I feel so excited about seeing my friends that I get butterflies inside! We do great things together that we enjoy, but we're all quite different to each other. I can tell my friends anything because I trust them. We do fall out sometimes, but we always make up and then it's fine.

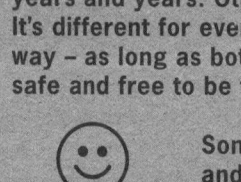

Well, kids. That all sounds like love.

But what is being "in love"? What's that like, Big Nan?

Being in love feels like a mixture of all the love feelings you've just told me about – all at once and all for one person!

Being in love can feel like a bit of a whirl to begin with, but it settles down into a special, warm, safe feeling where you feel like you can just be you. Some people take a long time to find someone special to love, while others find someone quite quickly.

Some people stay in love with the same person for years and years. Others have lots of little loves. It's different for everyone and there is no right way – as long as both people feel loved, respected, safe and free to be themselves.

Sometimes we just feel very excited and we think we love someone. But after a little while we realise it was a great feeling but it wasn't love. Love lasts longer. It changes as we change, but it doesn't go away.

32

www.fredandwoody.co.uk